Abuse

What's making you Stay

Prison's of the mind

Jennifer Turner

Author

Summary

My prayer is that you will experience while reading my book, the joy of "Letting Go" of the things that continues to imprison the mind and Inflict pain and agony to your life through a life of unforgiveness. Forgiveness is the healing balm for your mind body and soul. God wants to heal you everywhere you hurt. His desire for the reason that he came is that we live life and that we live it more abundantly.

That you would flourish in the fruits of the spirit of peace love joy happiness longsuffering etc. My desire is that you be made whole and come to the fullness of finding out the power that lies within you. You are somebody and you can do all things through Christ Jesus as you allow him to strengthen you. Through Prayer "ALL" things are possible when we believe we can receive.

Don't stay there, in the prison of your mind, don't wallow in shame don't get caught up in the web of pity and embarrassment when you can be free of the lies that the enemy is telling you that you can't be free of. It's how he keeps you trapped and bound in your mind. Hear the voice of the Lord reaching out to you through my book and be FREE.

I believe that if he did it for me, I know he will and can do the same for you. My life is a testimony of God goodness and his love toward us. All we have to do is be willing and obedient and we can eat the good of the land. I love you all with the love of God. Be Blessed.

Author Jennifer Turner

Dedication

This book is dedicated to all who have and will ever suffer for Abuse. Abusers have many faces and many reasons for why they are abusers. It could be family, friend, uncle's aunts, babysitters or lovers. My prayer is that you find the way of escape from the hands of someone who has been victimized and have not gotten the help they need to become Victorious. Always remember that Hurting people will only hurt others. Love does not cost it is freely given. Through acceptance of abuse whether physical verbal mental or emotionally you are agreeing knowingly or unknowingly to be

apart of an ongoing vicious cycle
of the offenders abusive actions.
You are not responsible for
someone else's pain. If you find
that you are or have become a
victim of Abuse of any type there
is a way out call the: National
Domestic Abuse Hotline 1-800-799-
7233 | 1-800-787-3224 (TTY) seek
out someone you can confide it
that will help you.

Most of All seek the spiritual
help through your local church
leader. You can be healed.

Acknowledgement
"Sticks and Stones "

I would like to acknowledge that the most damaging EFFECT OF ABUSE is Verbal. Now you might say "How So" but Sticks and Stones will break your bones but words, I have found personally and through spiritual counseling of many victims that "Words" are the most damaging because your bones will heal but words leave a long brutal and life last sting effect on its victim. Words such as; being called Stupid, Ugly, Fat ,

Use of the race card, Dummy, Fool, Good for nothing, a Mistake, Bald-head Sorry and the list goes on and on . Being told that you are good for nothing, you won't amount to anything, you will turn out just like you father/mother in the negative.

My God what a damaging and lasting effect that this makes on any individual any age, any race and gender. It's a working of the mind which the enemy desires to destroy even after the offender is gone. This is why we must seek out healing for our *Mind Body and our Souls.*

Table of Contents

1. In the Beginning.

2. Abuse has many ugly faces.

3. The spirit of Fear

4. What a man thinks, so is He

5. The Cry for help

6. The Reality's of Abuse

7. It's a battle for the Mind

8. God is well able

9. The Number one Question

10. So what's making you stay

11. Our healing starts with you

12. Yes You can Defeat that Giant

13. Getting past the Guilt

14. *God's desire*

15. Light at the end

16. Be healed from your Hurt

Chapter 1

"In the beginning"

As a child there was nowhere to
go and nothing I could possibly
do but to keep quiet about the
pain that was within me. Fear had
gripped me so that I thought
there was no help for me. You see
I was only thirteen and being
abused in many ways. Physically
mentally and emotionally
wondering! can anyone see my
pain? Knowing that I was too
young to handle it myself caused
me to think in the wrong manner.
No one loves me no one cares. The
ones you thought love you was the
offenders. Oh God; my mind was so
twisted and as an honor row
student my grades begin to
plummet. Imagine a thirteen year
old honor roll student being
advanced from the ninth grade to
twelfth grade after being given

an aptitude test in the eighties that advanced me early for graduation and my world came tumbling down because of abuse. It was as if I wanted to die. The pain of the offenses that I had to suffer was so unbearable for me that I though next to taking my own life, running away was the next best thing for me and so it was. If you have read my book *"Windows to my Soul"* it explains the struggles that I endured and the many pains I suffered at the hands of my abusers. What made me stay you may ask! I was a child with nowhere to go and no one I could tell my story to, No one to confide in. All alone bruise battered and yes broken and here I am now and over-comer through Christ writing that it may bless and help some man women boy or girl to let them know they are not alone. You don't have to stay in the prisons of your Mind.

Chapter 2

"Abuse has many ugly faces".

Abuse has many faces, comes in many ways, aimed in many directions, it is not racist, no one is omitted, it has no barriers, neither is it partial, it's for males and females adults & kids. "Abuse" how do I describe it? It comes from being told you will never be anything, you will be just like your daddy or mama and you will never have anything in life, being compared to others who have failed in life, or being tormented and bullied by other kids in school. Sometimes it comes from one's own self, after hearing these things repeated over and over the spirit to measure oneself up to or to comparison yourself to who you would want to be and that not who you are. Sizing you up to someone else it starts hiding within.

Tarring down your self-esteem from the ability to love and feel the normal embrace of those who suppose to love care and protect you to the state of the lack or desire to love and/or to be loved or even to being embraced by anyone. Fear of being left alone and the lack of accepting responsibility for oneself. Maybe from childhood living a life in the family of abuse, using the excuse my daddy did it, it's okay, mama did it "it's okay", *It's not okay.* These things cause you to become a prisoner one becomes locked up and a prisoner in your own mind. Free from the prison bars but bound in their own imprisonment.

Chapter 3

"God has not given us the spirit of Fear"

"Oh I'm afraid" is First off "fear" and it is of the devil and it comes in many forms, afraid of being alone. Afraid of being responsible of yourself or the lives of others such as your kids, that brings about a dependence upon someone else that causes you to except their abuse. "It's hard for me" is the next excuse that is use to cover up the real truth that fear causes you to except the abuse. Fear to step out to speaks up and to expose the abuser. Fear has brought an ending to many men and women boys and girls alike. Many have lost their lives through suicide with no way out thinking, no one will understand, no one loves me and the loss of hope. That thinking that causing them

to become "a prisoner in their own mind" and open the door to the devils attacks on the mind. Thinking that there is no way out but it doesn't have to be, there is hope and a way out, *it's not death*. The best kept secret ever is the one that you think you can't share with anyone out of fear. It is also the most dangerous and deadly one as well. There are warning signs but will anyone pay attention to them, will anyone help. Everyone don't know what you are going through or feeling, but if you would find that one you trust aside from God to openly share your experience with you can be healed but as long as you keep it in the dark (hidden) it gives power to the enemy of your mind cause you to continue to be bound in your mind taunting you in your sleep. Causing lost of sleep hot sweats and nightmares "It will haunt and only hurt you". You are not the offender; neither are you the cause of someone else's strongholds of offense. So why should you continue to suffer at the hands of your abuser. Make up your mind decide today I will no longer be a victim of my abuser *I will be Victorious*.

Chapter 4

"What a man thinks, so is He"

It's the way one thinks. Many suffer from abuse just because they think it okay, they think its love, they feel it their fault, their inadequate or incomplete in their own life. Abuse causes you to suffer at the hands of someone else who never got the help that they needed to be healed from their own wounds of abuse from life and they continue to struggle. They have many faces, the faces of *uncle aunt, mothers fathers sister brother cousin family friend baby sitters neighbor boyfriend* etc. But nothing and no one makes it right. *Abuse is the loss of control of your own self, the lost of one's own identity releasing the power of control to someone else to become the dominator of your life, causing*

you to become dependent giving
you fear and leaving you
helpless. That type of power only
belongs to God and even he does
not abuse us. We must first be
willing. He leaves the choice up
to us. There are many types and
forms of abuse mental physical
and emotional but two key factors
that lie within them all and it's
this, that it is meant to damage
and to destroy lives and not just
you but (without getting the help
needed) it will continue on and
on through-out the family). Being
abused is detrimental to anyone's
wellbeing due to the nature of
them, to anyone who allows it to
happen to them without speaking
out.

Chapter 5

"The Cry for help"

Sometime it is scary to open up and tell someone you need help. The thought of thinking what people will say is horrible and fearful alone. People will at time sum up the conclusion to the matter to say "It's your fault" that this has happened to you" you are lying, or at time deem you the victim as "no good" but nevertheless this offense did not happen to them. No matter what, *you did not deserve this*, no one does. Remember you are not alone, many have suffered some type of abuse or another and are afraid to tell someone. Whether at the hands of mother Family member boss neighbor or even close friends. It's time for you to be free of all the hurts that affect your mind and ability to function freely in life. The mind is a terrible thing when there is no peace. I remember in my first book "The Windows to my Soul" stating how afraid I was to tell anyone of my hurts as a young virgin girl being raped by my mother's friend s brother. With no one to talk to I cried trembling from within, it was a horrible and a very dark place for me. I thought I could never overcome this horrible attack on me and my body, yet I kept it all inside becoming a prisoner in my own mind, fearing no one would believe me. Being physically fondled by my grandfather, I thought surely I can't tell my mom this, "It's her father". I kept it in the dark place and the enemy continued to bind my mind with many thoughts of ending it all because I had no one to tell. You see anything kept in the dark only affects the carrier. It destroys the individual from within attacking the mind, the self-esteem, causing one to think less of them. Making you feel worthless. No matter what type of abuse it is, its effect is the same, its purpose is still the same and as long as you don't cry Out for Help it will continue to destroy you.

Chapter 6

"The Reality's is Abuse"

Abuse of any type imprisons the mind whether verbal physical spiritual and so on, it all carries a heavy weight of imprisonment on the mind. Feeling of shame low self-esteem loneliness incomplete worthlessness as well as loss of control One is in the prisons of their mind as one in a genuine prison the bar restraints. Limitation on where they can go and what they can do. Being controlled by the orders and regulations of another's power of authority which places limits on our lives And to be bound by the offenses of others is a very horrible place or should I say state of mind to be in. then one becomes ashamed and begin to feel the air of rejection by everyone they come in contact with family friends causing them to become withdrawn and inclusive leaving them at a total loss in life. I know been there done that. This is why I can personally attest to the fact that "Abuse" must stop. You have the power with God's help to make it so.

John 8:36 Therefore if the Son makes you free, you shall be free indeed. Allowing him to help you overcome the fear was one of the most awesome and powerfulliest things I could have done in my life. No one and nothing should have this ability to imprison us to the state of feeling worthless.

Chapter 7

"It's a battle for the Mind"

You have a destiny and a purpose full of dreams goals and aspirations that will affect the lives of many that look up to you. The enemy's desire is to abort you total life. It becomes a battle for your mind. The devil does not want you to reach your goals or to be happy. Jesus came that you might have life in *John 10:10 the thief does not come except to steal, and to kill, and to destroy. I have come that they may have life, and that they may have it more abundantly.* As long as we allow ourselves to live in fear of the giants of abuse in our lives we cannot live in that abundant life. When we are not healed we will tend to inflect this same pain and agony on others we love possibly our new husbands, wives, children and other family members and just imagine what you have had to undergo and place them in the same prison you are trying to free yourself of. This type of abuse trickles throughout ones family in many forms through mental verbal physical and sexual abuse. One's life become somewhat of a ticking time bomb waiting to explode at any moment. It causes you to suffer from lack of love for yourself causing you to seek it from others. It provokes you to have low self-esteem and having low-self-esteem leads to settling for second best or compromising your own desires. Losing your own identity it continues on to depression leading possibly to suicidal attempts that will eventually become successful in ultimately destroying you. It is the imprisonment of the mind. It will continue on as long as you allow it to remain without being heal from your hurts. You will become one that inflicts pain on the lives of others such as your children family member's friends etc. Abused people without help Abuses others. Fact is; it will cause you to seclude yourself off from everyone to become isolated or even possibly be in the room with many and yet seem like you are there all alone and that there is *"NO WAY OUT"*.

Chapter 8

"God is well able"

But God know the way through our wilderness experiences when we allow him to help us. He's not going to force you to do anything you are not willing to do, you must want his help. I find that it is certainly true that the mind is the greatest tool that the enemy uses to work against us in every way. Our ability to think is always under attack because if he (the devil) can keep us thinking negative we will never be able to reach our natural as well as our spiritual visions dreams or aspirations in life. Having the right mind is so very vital to our living and wellbeing this is why the bible tell us in

Phil 2:5 Let this mind be in you which were also in Christ

Jesus. We must put on the mind of Christ in order to overcome the trial that we have had to suffer in this life. That is what will make us an "Overcomer". Jesus makes it plan to us in his explanation to us of recognition in *John 10:10* the thief (devil) does not come except to steal, and to kill, and to destroy. I (Jesus) have come that they may have life, and that they may have it more abundantly. There is healing when we believe the word of God. He wants to deliver us from the strongholds and the imprisonments of our minds. They will pull you into many directions that you cannot handle.

Chapter 9

The Number one Question

"Why Me"

Why me? Is always the question that we ask ourselves before we start the blame syndrome then it becomes the excuse that we use to justify not excepting responsibility for ourselves and receiving the healing needed to make us victorious over the strong hold of abuse. It is the shortest and most common words used for the situation at hand "why me". Life has its way of causing you to use these words to humor the fact of any incident that affects us emotionally opening the door to our pity and sorrow emotions causing one to quickly be reminded of the offence. But remember you are not the offender you are the one that has been offended. The worst thing that can be done is that we go into a state of depression with the "why me" syndrome it will seem as though you are the only one that this has happen to but you are not alone. Many suffer with the hurt of the thought of being rejected if their offender is exposed rejected by family friends or people who just don't believe you. I truly can attest to being once a prisoner of my mind. Having to live life in fear of my offender I was afraid to tell anyone. Ashamed embarrassed and humiliated by my offender and the offense. To me all my innocence was taken from me I felt alone with no help and that I had no one to confide in. Fear had its grip on me. After being rapped verbally and physically abused. Today I am totally *Free Healed and delivered from the bondage* and imprisonment of my mind. I have been freed of the fear that gripped my thoughts. From being blinded by such horrible and tragic events that caused me to lose focus of who really I am. Today I consider myself a survivor and no longer a victim but am victorious. I have come to regain my own identity, know who I really am and to value love and appreciate me. Now I know you may say "What about my offender; I did to, but I focused on getting the help you needed for myself. Go ahead, forgive yourself even though you are not the offender and then forgive and expose your offender that the offenses won't happen to others and "Let it Go" so that you can be genuinely heal.

Chapter 10

"So what's making you stay?"

Is it the relentless lies you keep tell yourself as I did that he, she, it or they will change? Or that you are the one bringing this on yourself! Or the fact that this abuse that you are enduring is because they love you? Or is it the lust of your own fleshly desires (that kiss and make-up syndrome) really does it take a beat-down for one to show you that that love you. Is it the excuse of what happen to you when you were a child that brought about your low self esteem or the feeling that there is no one else that would love you? Hay!!!!! *What's making you Stay"?* "NOT SO". True love will never hurt you. Stop it, enough with the excuses that help you to remain in that situation. Don't you know that if you don't love yourself enough to put an end to this abusive situation it will continue in you? You will begin to abuse others such as your babies and it will continue in them and become one of the greatest horrors of family offense called generational curse that follows by example from generation to generation because no one will put a stop to it, It will continue on because you never did anything about it. Imagine your grand babies having to suffer the same thing you did at the hand of an abuser. Just what will you be able to tell them when they come to you for help?

Chapter 11

"Your healing starts with you"

No need to be ashamed. You have the power it's in you. Yes you can do it! You can be made whole. God will strengthen you for every task that is set before you to be free. Allow him to help you to break free of the chains that are holding you back in the Mind. He is ready willing and well able to help you. So go ahead; first, where there is responsibility on your part be healed. Take the responsibility for your actions. It may be that you unwarily did or said something to cause this offense, get God's forgiveness through repentance; then forgive yourself expose the abuse and the abuser and tell them you forgive them. Don't be afraid release yourself get your freedom from the torment the shame and the embarrassment of guilt that does not belong to you.

You can't have the victory of freedom until you first face up to the torment that lies within you from being the victim twice by the offense and then the torment that it continues to bring you through shame, embarrassment and unforgiveness. Be healed of your hurt, come out of the closet of your mind! You no longer have to be afraid. Let your cry for help be heard for the sake of the many others who have not come forth that are too afraid to tell someone. Turn your pressure into praise. God will give you freedom from the prison of your mind. Whom the son (Jesus) has set free they are free indeed.

Chapter 12

"Yes you can Defeat that Giant"

Defeat the giant of fear and step out by faith. It's only a giant because you continue to amplify it in fear. And as long as you keep it in the dark it will only hunt and hurt you, but you can do it. They are the giant monsters that hunt you in the night in your dreams you can hear the footsteps of your offender coming down you halls or through your windows chasing you again. Your heart began to race at an excessive speed for fear it will happen all over again Abuse.........but you can kill the giant so do it. It is okay to let go so that you can move forward. You have to be able to tell that giant "So what" it's over, I'm exposing you". God is well able to heal you every where you are hurting. He is waiting on you to be willing to let it go so that you can move forward. There is so much waiting on you to let go and live. Forgive and move forward there is nothing like being free totally.

Chapter 13

"Getting past the Guilt"

Move past the guilt and shame and
the embarrassment of your pass.
It is just that your pass. Let it
go before it kills you. Allow god
to help you become victorious oh
yes you can do it with the help
of the Lord. Start by calling
yourself what he has chosen you
to be; *1 Peter 2:9-10 But you are
a chosen generation, a royal
priesthood, a holy nation, His
own special people, that you may
proclaim the praises of Him who
called you out of darkness into
His marvelous light;* He is
calling you out of your dark
place out of the hurt and pain
into his marvelous light, so walk
in it with confidence in know
that he is and will always be
there for you to help you
overcome your pass. Paul stated
in;

Phil 3:13-14 Brethren, I do not count myself to have apprehended; but one thing I do, forgetting those things which are behind and reaching forward to those things which are ahead, 14 I press toward the goal for the prize of the upward call of God in Christ Jesus. You will never be able to move forward hold on to those pass offenses done against you or even that you have done. Forgive yourself and move forward. "Oh I know you might say it's not easy and it won't be but you can do it, it is attainable you can be free. Rid yourself of the pain and agony of defeat and you can become Victorious through Christ Jesus.

Phil 4:12-13 we can do all things through Christ who strengthens me. Just as he helped me he will do the same thing for you and you can move forward to

*bigger and a better way of
living.*

Chapter 14

"God desires so much more for us".

Let's look at what he says to us in; *3 John 2-3 "Beloved, I pray that you may prosper in all things and be in health, just as your soul prospers" First* let's look at what he calls us, his *"Beloved"* and the look at his desire, for us that we would *"Prosper"* and be in "Health" speaking in terms of our Total-Man and the only way that we can achieve that is that we free ourselves from all of our pass hurts and offenses through forgiveness, that we be released from the prisons of our mind. The stronghold that keeps us bound to the darkness and it keep us on lock-down a prisoner in the mind. We must know our worth to God, we are valuable and very important to him he even considers us as his own. *2 Cor 5:21 For He made Him who knew no sin to be sin for us, that we might become the righteousness of God in Him.* When we gain the knowledge of his desire for us and begin to grow in his word to follow his will for our lives we are considered his "The Righteousness of God" wow powerful. Our healing process begins when we know that we are precious to him no matter what we have been through and that he loves us so.

Chapter 15

"There is light at the end of every Tunnel"

Someone else's issue or struggles should not become your fault or reasoning for suffering. You should not have to suffer abuse at the hands of someone who has been abused and never sought help for their issues of it to become imprisoned in your mind. You are not the cause of their pain and though there may be a possibility that you can help them find their way, remember "Hurting people, Hurt other People". There is always a light at the end of any tunnel make your way to the light. When you see that you are unable to help an individual find your way of escape. Your end result could very well be your end if you remain in this unsafe Abusive environment. We were not created by the creator to suffer abuse at the hands of others when our creator loves us so, the word of god tell us in;

John 3:16 for God so loved the world that He gave His only begotten Son, that whoever believes in Him should not perish but have everlasting life. He loved us so that there is No Greater love then this. Jesus is the answer. Seek him while you have time. He will lead and direct you to the light, the pathway of escape. He will free you from the bondage and imprisonment of abuse and he "Will" heal you everywhere you hurt.

Chapter 16

"Be healed from your Hurt"

You can be healed through the power of the word of God from every dark place in your lives that continue to imprison your minds, causing you to live in fear. He is willing and well able to transform your hurt heal your heart and mind turning your life's tragedies into victories causing you to be an over comer with a powerful testimony that can help to free many others who has experienced the same things. *For Healing and Deliverance read: Isaiah 53:5 But He was wounded for our transgressions, He was bruised for our iniquities; The chastisement for our peace was upon Him, And by His stripes we are healed.*

Psalms 34:4

I sought the LORD, and He heard me,

*And delivered me from all my
fears*

Cry out to the Lord. Scream!!!!!!

Psalms 18:6
*In my distress I called upon the LORD,
and cried out to my God; He heard my
voice from His temple, and my cry came
before Him, even to His ears.*
Remember; Speak the Word and the
Word will speak for you.

About the Author

Jennifer Turner is a native of Houston, Texas. Her parents are Mr. Eddie & Lillie Winn. She is the ninth child of twelve. She accepted the Lord Jesus Christ as her personal savior at an early age. Later in life, she received a higher calling in ministry as a missionary and was later elevated to evangelist.

Shortly thereafter she united in holy matrimony with the late great, Bishop Jerry Turner. Where the birthing of their church was formed to be Genesis Tabernacle of Love COGIC Interdenominational Inc. and she became the Pastor under the leadership of her husband. There they worked together to build discipleship in the lives of others. She is the *General Supervisor* in the *COGIC*

Interdenominational, Inc. Organization of the Women's Work in St. Louis, MO.

Upon the passing of Bishop Turner in 2013 she was appointed Overseer of GTOL COGIC Interdenominational Inc, as well as Sunrise Family Worship Center and God's Way Ministry. She is a spiritual counselor, advisor, administrator of her church and has been for the past twenty-one years

She is the founder of the *Sister to Sister Women & Children Organization* as well as the *Total Man Food Pantry* located in the city of Rosenberg, Texas. In January of 2015 she gave birth to the *Words of Wisdom* (W.O.W.) forum. The forum is an open discussion where people of God can dialogue about life issues and receive biblical wisdom. Jennifer Turner is an established author and publisher of her book "Windows to my Soul". She is spreading her global message of faith healing and deliverance to all. She believes that there is a mandated on her life and that this is her passion this is who she is.

NOTES

www.ingramcontent.com/pod-product-compliance
Lightning Source LLC
Chambersburg PA
CBHW072039060426
42449CB00010BA/2344